IN THE PARK

David M. Schwartz *is an award-winning author of children's books, on a wide variety of topics, loved by children around the world.* Dwight Kuhn's *scientific expertise and artful eye work together with the camera to capture the awesome wonder of the natural world.*

For a free color catalog describing Gareth Stevens Publishing's list of high-quality books and multimedia programs, call 1-800-542-2595 (USA) or 1-800-461-9120 (Canada). Gareth Stevens Publishing's Fax: (414) 225-0377.

Library of Congress Cataloging-in-Publication Data

Schwartz, David M.
    In the park / by David M. Schwartz; photographs by Dwight Kuhn.
       p. cm. — (Look once, look again)
    Includes bibliographical references (p. 23) and index.
    Summary: Explores the world of pigeons, rabbits, squirrels, swans, and
other animals living among the grass and burdocks of a park.
    ISBN 0-8368-2243-9 (lib. bdg.)
    1. Urban animals—Juvenile literature. 2. Urban plants—Juvenile literature.
3. Parks—Juvenile literature. [1. Urban animals.] I. Kuhn, Dwight, ill.
II. Title. III. Series: Schwartz, David M. Look once, look again.
QL49.S27497 1998
591.75'6—dc21   98-6311

This North American edition first published in 1999 by
Gareth Stevens Publishing
1555 North RiverCenter Drive, Suite 201
Milwaukee, Wisconsin 53212 USA

First published in the United States in 1997 by Creative Teaching Press, Inc., P.O. Box 6017, Cypress, California, 90630-0017.

Text © 1997 by David M. Schwartz; photographs © 1997 by Dwight Kuhn. Additional end matter © 1999 by Gareth Stevens, Inc.

Printed in the United States of America

1 2 3 4 5 6 7 8 9 03 02 01 00 99

IN THE PARK

by David M. Schwartz

photographs by Dwight Kuhn

A SPRINGBOARDS INTO

SCIENCE

SERIES

Gareth Stevens Publishing

MILWAUKEE

If you were a worm, these would look like giant blades, reaching high into the sky.

If no one cuts these blades of grass, they will grow tall and little flowers will appear. At the park, however, someone mows the grass, and it becomes a bright green lawn instead.

These teeth are
sharp and strong,
but they are not
made to bite you —
unless you're a nut!

With their sharp teeth, gray squirrels crack open acorns and other nuts. They also eat seeds and fruit.

Squirrels must chew on hard objects to keep their front teeth from growing too long.

8

This is not a marble. It is the eye of a bird that everybody knows.

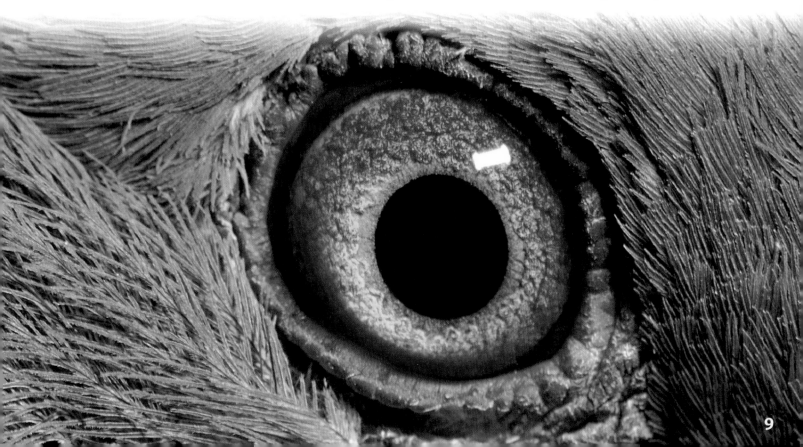

Some pigeons
stay in one place,
in a park, most
of their lives.
Other pigeons,
though, fly
thousands of miles
(kilometers) to find
their way home.

This bushy tail belongs to a masked rascal that loves to explore.

LOOK AGAIN

Raccoons are curious and clever. Their paws have five long fingers, just like your hands. With their fingers, raccoons find yummy things to eat.

12

If you think these are hooks, you are right.
Walk near them, and they will hook onto you!

Burdock seeds have lots of little hooks that grab your clothing as you walk by. When an animal passes by, the seeds stick to its fur. This is how some types of seeds are carried to a new place.

14

A children's fairy tale has an "ugly duckling" that grows up to be an elegant ...

...swan. With its long neck, a graceful swan reaches down to find its food. It grasps underwater plants in its wide, flat bill. Then, it pulls the plants up from the bottom of the pond.

This is a nail at the
end of a furry foot.
Whose foot could it be?

With her front feet, a cottontail
rabbit mother digs a nest.
She scoops up dirt and carves
a "bowl" in the ground.
She lines it with grass,
leaves, and soft fur
from her coat.

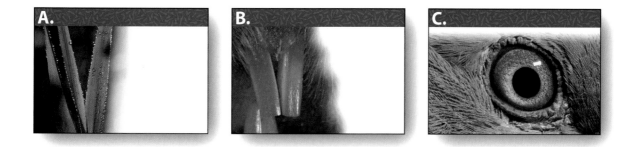

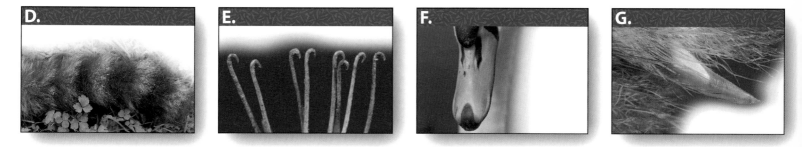

Look closely. Can you name these plants and animals?

A. Grass

B. Gray squirrel

C. Pigeon

D. Raccoon

E. Burdock seeds

F. Swan

G. Cottontail rabbit

How many were you able to identify correctly?

blades: in the grass family, thin and narrow leaves of grass.

burdock: a plant with large, broad leaves and bristly seeds. Seeds of the burdock "hitchhike" to a new location when they stick to fur or clothing.

bushy: full and thick. Some animals, such as raccoons, have bushy tails.

clever: having or showing a quick mind; smart.

curious: eager to find out about something.

duckling: a young duck.

elegant: graceful and beautiful, like the movement of a swan.

explore: to go into or travel through an unknown place for the purpose of discovery.

graceful: able to move around easily and smoothly.

grasps: grabs and holds tightly.

marble: a little ball made of glass that is used in some types of children's games.

masked: wearing or seeming to wear a disguise on the face. The raccoon has a masked face.

mows (v): cuts down grass or other plants.

rascal: a mischievous animal or person.

scoop (v): to dig out or take up with a dipping action. The cottontail rabbit scoops dirt to make a nest, which it lines with grass, leaves, and fur.

underwater: beneath the surface of the water.

ACTIVITIES

It's All in the Family!

Squirrels, which can be commonly seen in backyards and city parks, are members of the rodent family. Like other rodents, they have sharp teeth for gnawing, or chewing, on hard seeds and nuts. Find out about the other kinds of rodents that live in North America. Which is the biggest rodent? Which is the smallest? Make a list of the ways that the various types of rodents are alike. Then, list the ways the various types of rodents are different.

Burdock Sculpture

A burdock seed "hitchhikes" to a new location where it can grow as a new plant. Find some burdock plants in a park or your own backyard. Can you see the individual seeds and their hooks? Stick several burdock seeds together to make a sculpture of a person or animal.

Be a Nature Detective

Go for a walk in a park and look for clues that animals have been there. Can you find any tracks in the mud or snow? What animal do you think made the tracks? Find a book on animal tracks at the library to help you solve the mystery. Raccoons have paws that look like little hands. This makes raccoon tracks easy to identify.

Color Hunt

Look through an old magazine that has lots of color pictures. Cut out a small sample of at least ten different colors. Paste or glue the color samples onto a piece of cardboard. If you'd like, use a pair of scissors to cut the cardboard in the shape of an artist's palette. Take the palette with you on a walk through a park. Can you find objects or animals in the park that match each of the ten different colors?

More Books to Read

Birds. Young Scientist Concepts & Projects (series). Jen Green (Gareth Stevens)

The Nature and Science of Seeds. Exploring the Science of Nature (series).
    Jane Burton and Kim Taylor (Gareth Stevens)

Pigeons and Doves. Ray Rofsinger (Childrens Press)

Raccoon Magic for Kids. Animal Magic for Kids (series). Jeff Fair (Gareth Stevens)

Seeds Get Around. Nancy White (Newbridge Communications)

Squirrels and Chipmunks. Allan Fowler (Childrens Press)

Videos

Animals in the City. (Encyclopædia Britannica Educational Corporation)

The Rabbit. (Barr Films)

Squirrel on My Shoulder. (Public Media)

Web Sites

www.nps.gov/parks.html

www.loomcom.com/raccoons/

Some web sites stay current longer than others. For further web sites, use your search engines to locate the following topics: *parks, pigeons, rabbits, raccoons, seeds, squirrels,* and *swans.*

INDEX